This Book
BELONGS
to

For
Pat

PUBLISHED IN 2021 by

LAURENCE KING PUBLISHING Ltd
361 - 373 CITY ROAD
LONDON EC1V 1LR
Tel + 44 20 7841 6900

www.laurenceking.com
enquiries@laurenceking.com

A CATALOG RECORD OF THIS BOOK IS AVAILABLE
FROM THE BRITISH LIBRARY.

ISBN 978-1-78627-7-725

Printed in China

Thank You

LAURENCE KING
DONALD DINWIDDIE
LEAH WILLEY
FELICITY AWDRY
ELIZABETH SHEINKMAN P.F.D

ANGUS HYLAND
Hamish & Alexander

VANESSA GREEN
@theurbanant

Marion Deuchars

Let's make some GREAT ART
COLORS

LAURENCE KING

ART MATERIALS

A LIST OF BASIC ART MATERIALS

WHITE GLUE (OR GLUE STICK)

SCISSORS

CONSTRUCTION PAPER
(in different sizes and colors)

RULER

PENCILS

COLORED PENCILS

PENS

ACRYLIC PAINT PENS

TAPE

PAINT BRUSHES (different sizes)

CRAYONS OR PASTELS

PAINTS

DRAWING COMPASS

ERASER

PENCIL SHARPENER

WATER CONTAINER

INK

INK PADS

PENCILS

PENCILS COME IN ALL SHAPES AND SIZES. HARD, SOFT AND WATER SOLUBLE.

WHITE ACRYLIC PAINT PEN

VERY USEFUL FOR ADDING HIGHLIGHTS AND DRAWING WHITE ON TOP OF BLACK.

CHALKS AND PASTELS

COME IN BEAUTIFUL COLORS. THEY HAVE A PAINTING-EFFECT WHEN YOU MIX OR BLEND THEM.

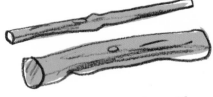

CHARCOAL IS SOFT, BLACK, AND VELVET-LIKE TO DRAW WITH.

ERASERS

REGULAR ERASER (HARD)

PUTTY ERASER (SOFT)

CAN BE SQUEEZED INTO SHAPES.

FELT-TIP PENS

COME IN ALL DIFFERENT SHAPES AND SIZES. TRY TO GET SOME THICK AND THIN ONES.

BRUSH PENS ARE USEFUL TOO ↗

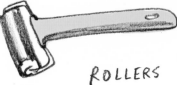

ROLLERS

ARE GREAT FOR PAINTING LARGE AREAS. OR USE ONE TO MAKE YOUR OWN COLORED PAPER.

DRAWING COMPASS

PAINTS

ACRYLIC is a plastic-based paint. Mix with water to use it thick or thin. Very versatile.

GOUACHE is an opaque watercolor paint.
You cannot see the white of the paper through it.

POSTER/CRAFT paint is ideal for posters, crafts, and school projects. It is a water-based paint and the least expensive to buy.

PAN or TUBE WATERCOLOR

WATERCOLOR is a transparent paint; you can see the white of the paper through it

PAPER

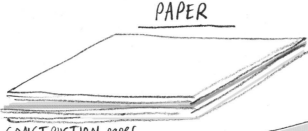

CONSTRUCTION paper
PHOTOCOPY paper
CARTRIDGE paper
(comes in different weights/ thickness
80 gsm - light (ok for DRAWING)
300 gsm - heavy (ok for paint)

INK IS GREAT FOR DRAWING. IT COMES IN ALL DIFFERENT COLOURS.

USE A "DIP PEN", BRUSH, STICK, OR CARD!

ROUND

FLAT

POINTED

A good pair of SHARP SCISSORS. You can also buy safety scissors.

BRUSHES
HOG/BRISTLE - hard brushes, good for acrylic and poster paints.
SYNTHETIC - cheaper but good all rounders (all paints).
SABLE - Soft. Expensive but high quality (all paints).

PALETTES
GOOD FOR MIXING AND STORING PAINT.

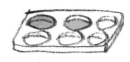

PLASTIC PALETTES

PAPER PALETTES ARE VERY USEFUL. THEY ARE DISPOSABLE. AND YOU CAN KEEP PAINT WET FOR A FEW DAYS BY PUTTING A PAPER TOWEL ON TOP.

MASKING TAPE

OLD JARS ARE GOOD AS WATER JARS

GLUE IS GOOD IN A GLUE STICK, OR USE PVA (WHITE GLUE)

WHITE PVA GLUE

VERY USEFUL FOR TAPING PAPER TO DESK. ALSO FOR HIDING OR "MASKING" AREAS ON THE PAPER.

MAKE A
COLOR WHEEL

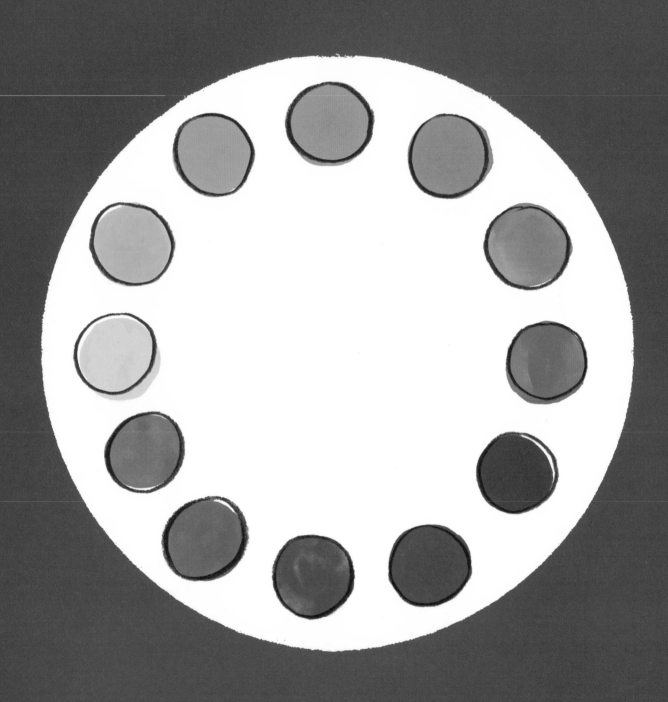

COLOR IN WITH FELT-TIP PENS OR COLORED PENCILS.

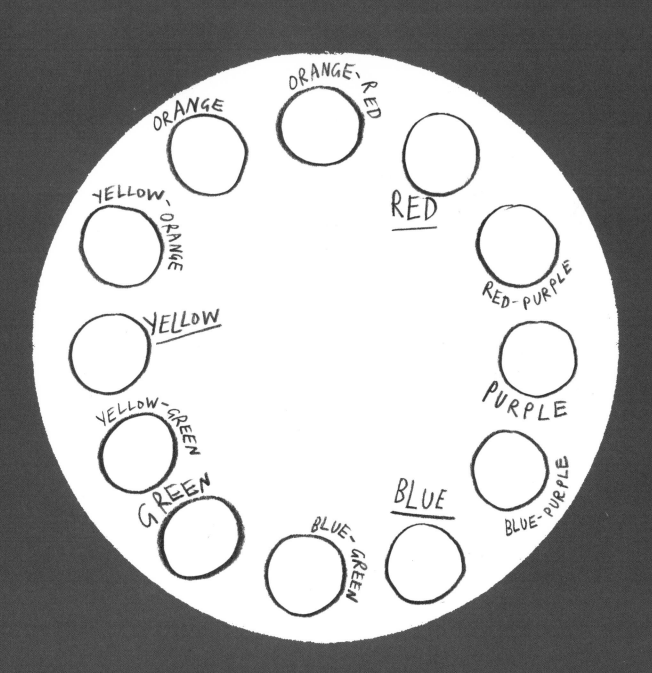

PRIMARY COLORS

THESE ARE CALLED PRIMARY BECAUSE THEY CANNOT BE MADE BY MIXING OTHER COLORS TOGETHER.

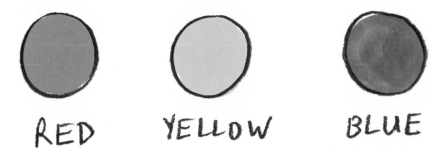

RED   YELLOW   BLUE

SECONDARY COLORS

THESE ARE MADE BY MIXING TWO OF THE PRIMARY COLORS TOGETHER. THEY ARE:

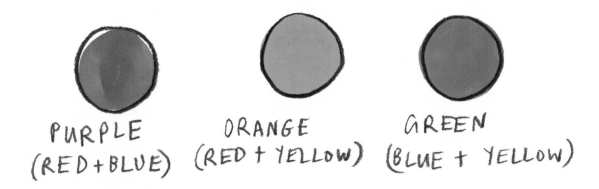

PURPLE   ORANGE   GREEN
(RED + BLUE)   (RED + YELLOW)   (BLUE + YELLOW)

USING PAINT OR FELT-TIP PENS OR COLORED PENCILS, PRACTISE
MIXING YOUR PRIMARY COLORS TO MAKE SECONDARY COLORS.

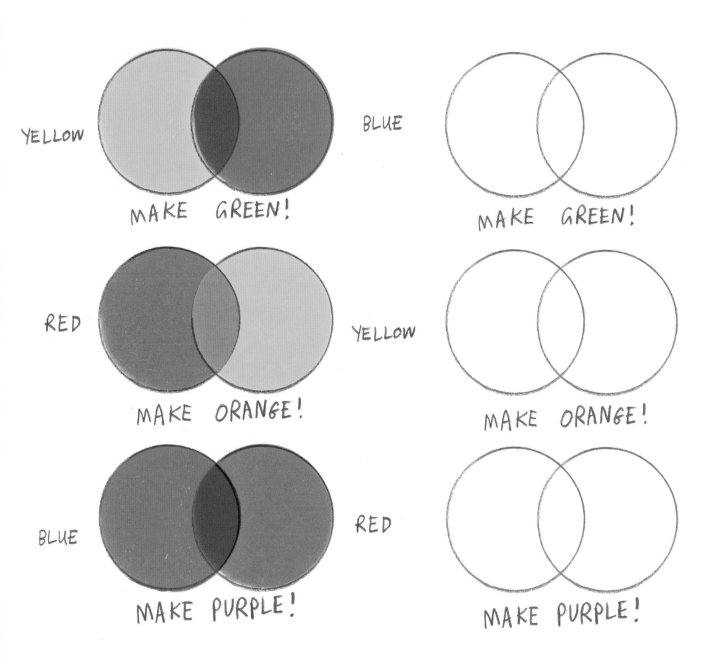

YELLOW   BLUE
MAKE GREEN!   MAKE GREEN!

RED   YELLOW
MAKE ORANGE!   MAKE ORANGE!

BLUE   RED
MAKE PURPLE!   MAKE PURPLE!

CARMINE RED

THE COLOR CARMINE RED IS
PRODUCED FROM "Cochineal."
COCHINEAL IS A TINY INSECT FROM
SOUTH AMERICA. 70,000 INSECTS
NEED TO BE CRUSHED and DRIED
TO PRODUCE 1 lb of COCHINEAL DYE.

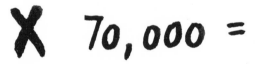 X 70,000 = 1 lb CARMINE RED

COLOR IN THIS BIRD
called a ROBIN (red breast).

COLOR IN THESE PLANT-LIKE
SHAPES IN BRIGHT COLORS.

COMPLEMENTARY COLORS

ARE OPPOSITE COLORS ON THE COLOR WHEEL.

RED – GREEN
ORANGE – BLUE
YELLOW – PURPLE

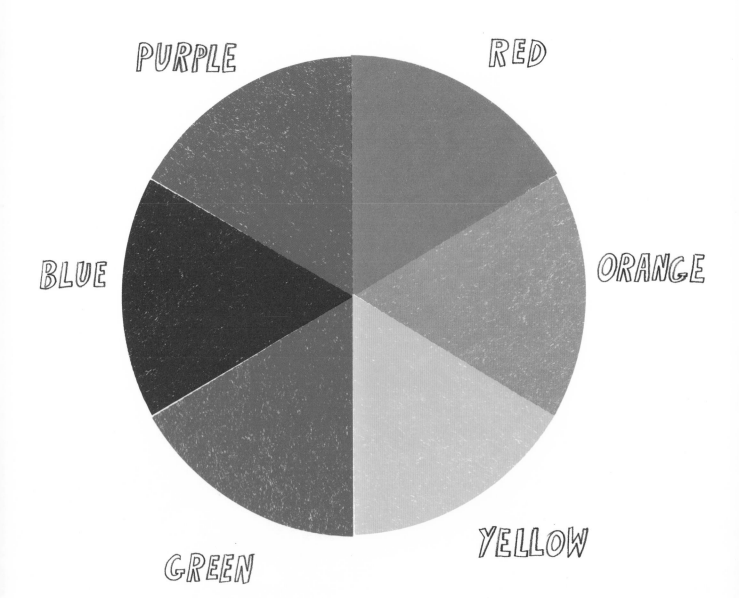

MAKE COMPLEMENTARY COLOR TREES.

<u>WHAT YOU NEED</u>

COLOR INK PADS

OR YOU COULD MIX UP THE COLORS IN GOUACHE OR ACRYLIC PAINT AND DO FINGER PAINTING. FINGERS!

RED - GREEN

ORANGE - BLUE

YELLOW - PURPLE

FINGERPRINT OR FINGERPAINT LEAVES USING
COMPLEMENTARY COLORS.

RED — GREEN

ORANGE — BLUE

YELLOW — PURPLE

ORANGE

THE COLOR ORANGE WAS
NAMED <u>AFTER</u> THE FRUIT.
IN ENGLISH, THE COLOR
USED TO BE CALLED
YELLOW-RED,
WHICH IS EXACTLY WHAT IT
IS: A MIXTURE OF
YELLOW AND RED

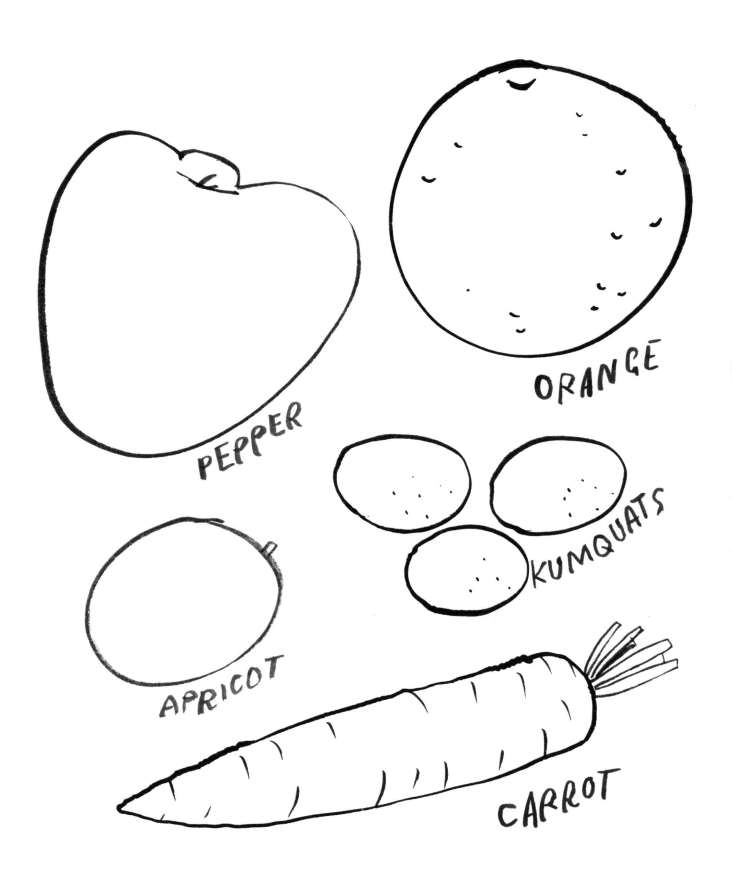

PEPPER

ORANGE

KUMQUATS

APRICOT

CARROT

CAN YOU COLOR IN THE ORANGE-
COLORED FRUITS AND VEGETABLES?

COLOR AND MOOD

DESIGN A PATTERN FOR EACH COLOR THAT REFLECTS HOW YOU FEEL ABOUT IT.

HERE IS HOW I FEEL ABOUT RED, YELLOW, AND BLUE.

_RED _____

_YELLOW _____

_BLUE _____

HOW DO YOU FEEL ABOUT EACH OF THESE COLORS?

- GREEN _____

- PURPLE _____

- BLACK _____

YOUR
FAVORITE COLOR _____

COLOR IN THE RED APPLE AND YELLOW GRAPEFRUIT.
SEE IF YOU CAN USE DIFFERENT SHADES OF RED AND YELLOW.

COLOR CODES

WE OFTEN USE COLOR TO HELP US IDENTIFY SIMILAR OBJECTS.
HERE ARE SOME EXAMPLES:

COLOR THE OBJECTS BELOW BASED ON HOW YOU
IMAGINE THEM TO LOOK ACCORDING TO THEIR LABELS.

USE COLORED PENCILS OR PENS.

ILL

ANGRY

DANGEROUS

SAFE

HOT

COLD

ORANGE JUICE

LEMONADE

FALL

SUMMER

FRESH APPLE

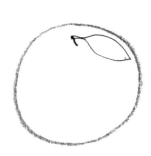

MOLDY APPLE

SUN

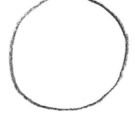

MOON

BUTTERFLY

MOTH

BROWN

IS MADE BY MIXING RED, BLUE, AND YELLOW.

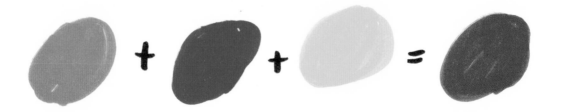

LEONARDO DA VINCI USED BROWN INK MADE FROM THE INK SACS OF CUTTLEFISH TO DRAW AND WRITE WITH.

COLOR IN THIS BROWN BEAR.

BEARS ARE OMNIVORES, WHICH MEANS
THEY EAT BOTH PLANTS AND ANIMALS.

COLOR IN THIS BALLOON DOG
SCULPTURE IN BRIGHT COLORS.

PAINT A RAINBOW HEART

MATERIALS NEEDED

POSTER PAINT
PAPER
BRUSHES
PAINT TRAY OR
PAPER CUPS

1. FOLD A PIECE OF PAPER IN HALF, OPEN IT OUT, AND ON ONE SIDE PAINT HALF A HEART SHAPE.

2. BEFORE IT DRIES, QUICKLY FOLD THE PAPER BACK AND PRESS FIRMLY.

3. OPEN TO REVEAL A "COMPLETE" HEART SHAPE. WAIT FOR IT TO DRY.

4. CONTINUE THE PROCESS UNTIL YOU HAVE COMPLETED THE 7 RAINBOW COLORS. EACH HALF RAINBOW YOU PAINT WILL GET SMALLER EACH TIME.

HANDY TIP

MIX UP ALL YOUR PAINTS BEFORE STARTING, WITH A DIFFERENT BRUSH FOR EACH COLOR.

LOOKING AT COLOR

CAN YOU DRAW AND COLOR SOME NEW OBJECTS?

CAN YOU DRAW AND COLOR THINGS THAT ARE RED?

CAN YOU DRAW AND COLOR THINGS THAT ARE YELLOW?

CAN YOU DRAW AND COLOR THINGS THAT ARE BLUE?

CAN YOU DRAW AND COLOR THINGS THAT ARE GREEN?

YELLOW
OCHER

YELLOW OCHER IS THE OLDEST YELLOW. THE OCHER CLAY IS MINED FROM THE GROUND, WASHED TO SEPARATE THE SAND FROM THE OCHER, THEN DRIED IN THE SUN.

YELLOW IS ASSOCIATED WITH ILLNESS, COWARDICE, and CAUTION, BUT ALSO UNIVERSALLY WITH THE SUN.

COLOR IN THE YELLOW TANG FISH.

IT IS A SALT WATER FISH FROM THE SOUTH PACIFIC OCEAN NEAR HAWAII. IT HAS 2 WHITE SPIKES ON THE SIDES OF ITS TAIL. IT WILL USE THEM TO "STAB" ANOTHER FISH IF ATTACKED.

ADD SOME COLORED LEAVES TO SHOW THE SEASONS.

SPRING

FALL

SUMMER

WINTER

COLOR IN THIS MODERN ART MUSEUM.

COLOR AND MASKING TAPE

MAKE A GREAT DESIGN WITH TAPE AND CRAYONS.

WHAT YOU NEED

MASKING TAPE OR REMOVABLE TAPE
PAPER
CRAYONS
SCISSORS

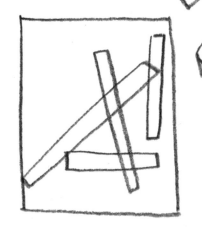

1. STICK STRIPS OF TAPE ONTO YOUR PAPER. YOU CAN PLACE IT IN STRAIGHT LINES OR DIAGONALLY. OVERLAP THE TAPE.

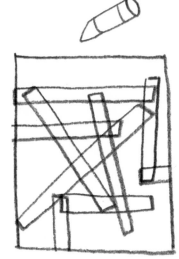

2. COLOR THE WHITE SPACES LEFT ON THE PAPER WITH CRAYONS.

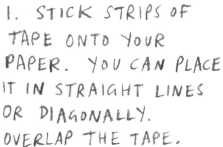

3. CAREFULLY PEEL OFF THE TAPE TO REVEAL YOUR DESIGN.

MALACHITE GREEN

THE ANCIENT EGYPTIANS USED TO CRUSH MALACHITE (A GREEN MINERAL) TO MAKE THE COLOR GREEN. A PAINT-BOX WITH THIS COLOR WAS FOUND IN THE TOMB OF TUTANKHAMUN!

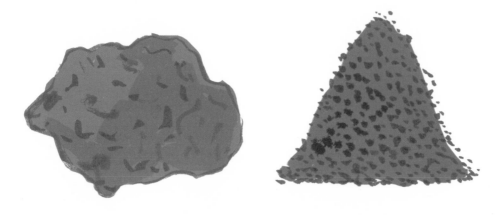

GREEN EYES IN HUMANS ARE VERY
RARE BUT NOT IN TABBY CATS.
COLOR IN THE KITTEN.

MULTI-COLOR

THERE IS A WAY YOU CAN CREATE A MULTI-COLORED COPY OF A DRAWING.
THIS EFFECT NEVER TURNS OUT THE SAME WAY TWICE!

WHAT YOU NEED

TWO SHEETS OF PAPER
CRAYONS
A SOFT PENCIL
TWO PAPER CLIPS (OR REMOVABLE)
    TAPE

1. TAKE ONE OF THE SHEETS OF PAPER AND
   COVER THE ENTIRE SURFACE WITH PATCHES
   OF MANY DIFFERENT COLORS USING THE
   CRAYONS.

2. PLACE THE SECOND SHEET ON TOP
   OF THE COLORED PIECE OF PAPER.

3. USE PAPER CLIPS (OR TAPE) TO SECURE
   THE TWO SHEETS TOGETHER
   DRAW SOME DESIGNS ON THE
   TOP SHEET OF PAPER.

4. WHEN YOU ARE DONE, TAKE OFF THE
   CLIPS AND REMOVE THE TOP SHEET
   AND TURN IT OVER.

* WHATEVER YOU DRAW WILL BE PRINTED ON THE REVERSE OF THE TOP SHEET IN THE COLORS
OF THE CRAYON PATCHES ON THE SHEET BELOW.

DRAWINGS

YOU'VE NOW GOT A MULTI-COLORED VERSION OF YOUR DRAWING!

COMBINING COLORS

THERE ARE MANY WAYS OF COMBINING COLORS OTHER THAN "MIXING" THEM. HERE'S WHAT I'VE DONE WITH COLORED PENCILS AND FELT-TIP PENS.

BELOW DRAW YOUR OWN STACKING SHAPES. BUILD THEM UP,
PIECE BY PIECE, LIKE DOODLING, THEN COLOR IN.

LAPIS (BLUE) LAZULI

DURING THE Renaissance LAPIS LAZULI ROCKS WERE CRUSHED INTO POWDER AND MIXED WITH OIL TO MAKE AN INTENSE BLUE.

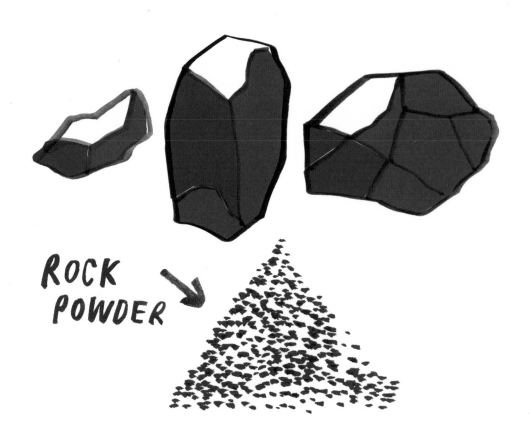

ROCK POWDER

LAPIS LAZULI WAS MORE EXPENSIVE THAN GOLD.

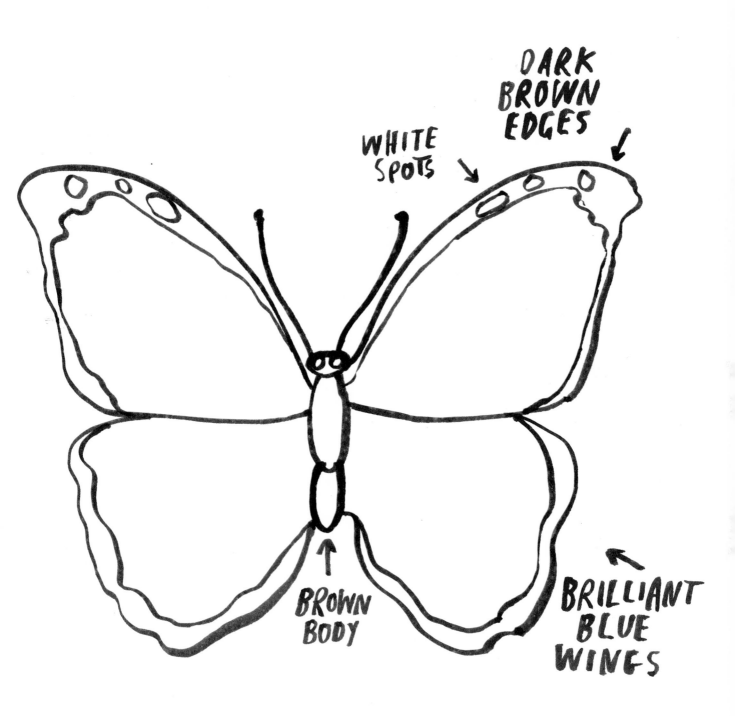

WHITE SPOTS

DARK BROWN EDGES

BROWN BODY

BRILLIANT BLUE WINGS

COLOR IN THIS BLUE MORPHO **BUTTERFLY.**

THIS STRANGE-COLORED POT PLANT
HAS GROWN SO HUGE THAT IT'S
GROWING OUT OF THE WINDOW.
CAN YOU DRAW IT AND COLOR IT IN?

PAINT OR COLOR THIS CHAMELEON
SO THAT IT IS LOST IN THE BACKGROUND,
MAKING IT CAMOUFLAGED.

RED

ORANGE

YELLOW

GREEN

BLUE

INDIGO

VIOLET

MATCH THE RAINBOW COLORS TO THE WORDS.
THEN COLOR THEM IN.

TYRIAN PURPLE

THOUSANDS of PURPURA SNAILS WERE CRUSHED TO PRODUCE THIS HIGHLY PRIZED PIGMENT OF THE ANCIENT WORLD.

CLEOPATRA ORDERED THOUSANDS OF SNAILS TO BE CRUSHED to make a A FEW PRECIOUS OUNCES.

COLOR CLEOPATRA WITH PURPLE.

CRAYON ETCHING

MAKE A CRAYON ETCHING. IT IS VERY SIMPLE TO DO.

WHAT YOU NEED

- WHITE CARD
- CRAYONS (BRIGHT COLORS)
- BLACK GOUACHE
  OR ACRYLIC PAINT
- 2H PENCIL
  OR COCKTAIL STICK
  OR SHARP TOOL
- PAPER TOWEL
- FLAT PAINTBRUSH

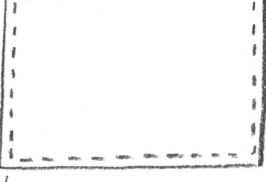

1. DRAW A BORDER ON WHITE CARD.

2. COLOR THE CARD WITH CRAYONS UP TO YOUR BORDER, LEAVING NO WHITE SPACES. RUB AWAY SURPLUS WAX WITH PAPER TOWEL.

3. PAINT OVER CRAYON WITH BLACK ACRYLIC OR GOUACHE PAINT WITH A WIDE, FLAT BRUSH. COVER EVENLY. PAINT SHOULD BE QUITE THICK BUT NOT LUMPY.

4. SCRAPE YOUR PATTERN INTO THE BLACK PAINT TO REVEAL THE CRAYON COLOURS. RUB AWAY SURPLUS DRIED PAINT.

WATERCOLOR BLOB FLOWERS

1. WET THE PAPER

WATER

WATERCOLORS OR INKS

2. DROP A WATERCOLOR BLOB ONTO WET PAPER.

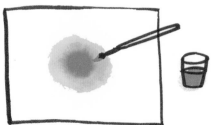

3. ADD ANOTHER SMALLER COLOR BLOB ONTO THE FIRST COLOR BEFORE IT DRIES.

NOW MAKE YOUR OWN WATERCOLOR FLOWERS HERE.

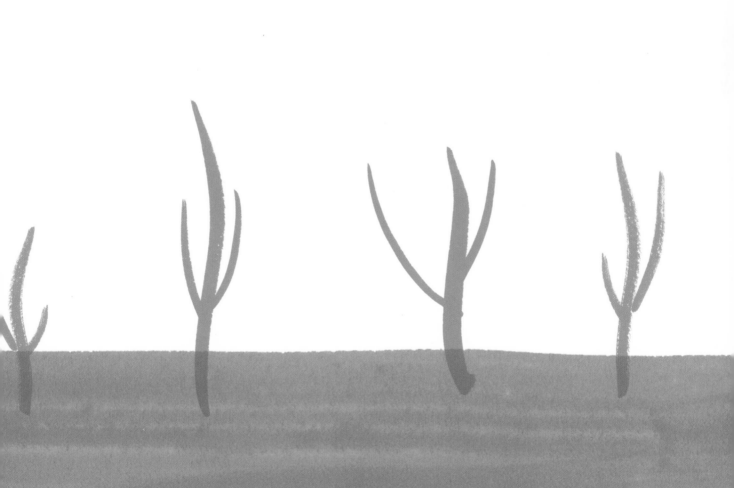

COPY THE RAINBOW COLORS
IN THIS SQUARE GRID PATTERN.

TRY DIFFERENT COLORS IN THE
SQUARE GRID.

TRY MAKING YOUR OWN HERE. ↙

TRY MAKING YOUR OWN HERE. ↙

PINK

PINK IS A PALE SHADE OF RED. YOU CAN MAKE IT BY MIXING RED AND WHITE TOGETHER.

THE COLOR PINK HAS BEEN DESCRIBED IN STORIES SINCE ANCIENT TIMES. A FAMOUS STORY CALLED "THE ODYSSEY" BY THE GREEK POET HOMER USED IT TO DESCRIBE THE MORNING SKY.

COLOR IN THE PINK FLAMINGO.

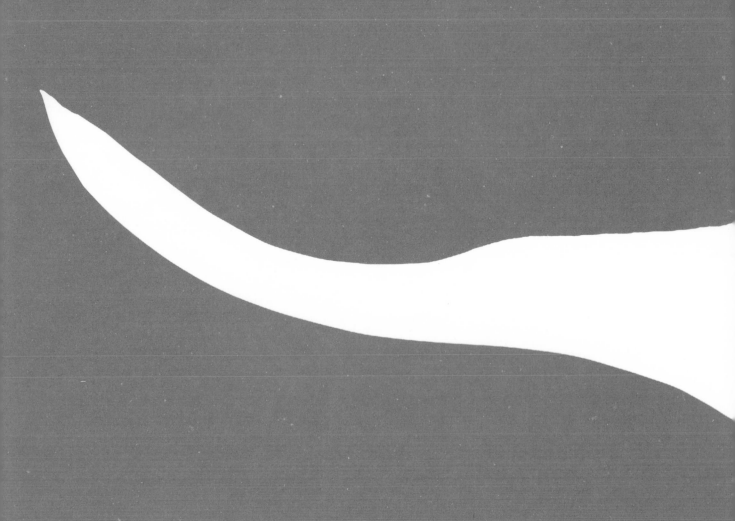

COLOR THE VELOCIRAPTOR IN GREEN.

SPINNING TOP

WHAT YOU NEED

CARD

SCISSORS

OR
PAINTS
PENS
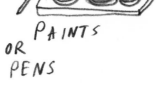

A COMPASS
OR A JAR
LID TO
MAKE THE
CIRCLE SHAPE
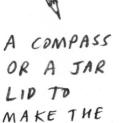

SHORT
PENCIL

1.

CUT OUT A CIRCLE
OF CARD.
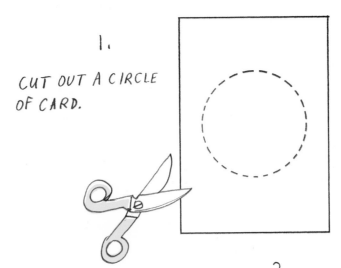

2.

DECORATE WITH
PAINT, PENS, OR
STICKERS.
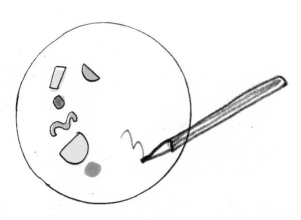

3.

MAKE A HOLE IN THE CENTER
AND PUSH A SHORT PENCIL THROUGH.

4.

SPIN THE TOP.
WHAT HAPPENS TO THE COLORS?

TRY MAKING YOUR OWN SPINNING TOP.

GRAY

IS A COLOR BETWEEN BLACK AND WHITE.
THERE ARE MANY SHADES OF GRAY.

BLACK + (WHITE) = GRAY

A PENCIL HAS GRAY LEAD.
YOU CAN MAKE YOUR PENCIL GO FROM
DARK GRAY TO LIGHT GRAY BY PRESSING
IT FROM HARD TO LIGHT.

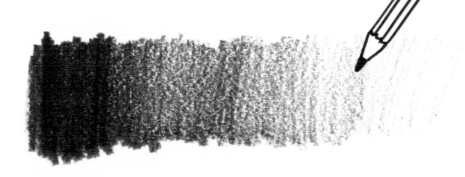

GRAY IS A VERY COMMON COLOR FOR
ANIMALS, BIRDS, AND FISH. IT IS THE
PERFECT COLOR FOR CAMOUFLAGE, ALLOWING
THEM TO BLEND INTO THEIR SURROUNDINGS.

COLOR IN THIS GRAY ARMADILLO.

WARM AND COLD COLORS

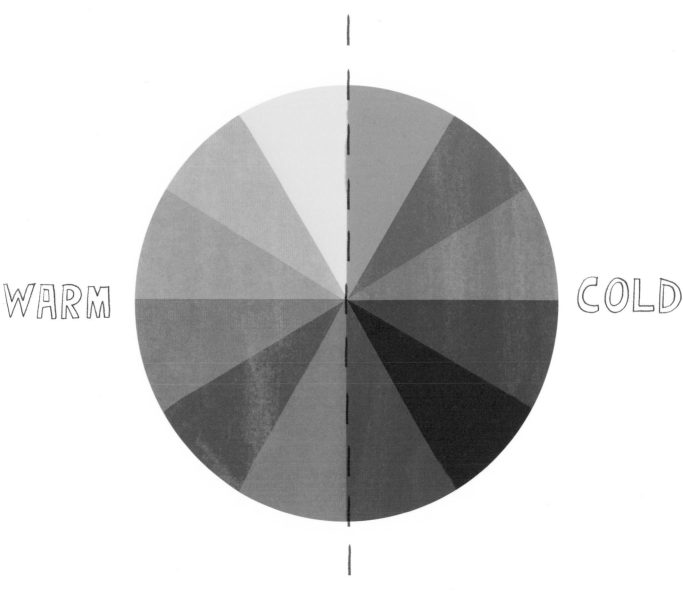

WARM

COLD

USING THE COLOR CHART,
COLOR IN THE OPPOSITE PAGE
USING **COLD** COLORS FOR THE
BACKGROUND SHAPES AND **WARM**
COLORS FOR THE STAR SHAPE.

→

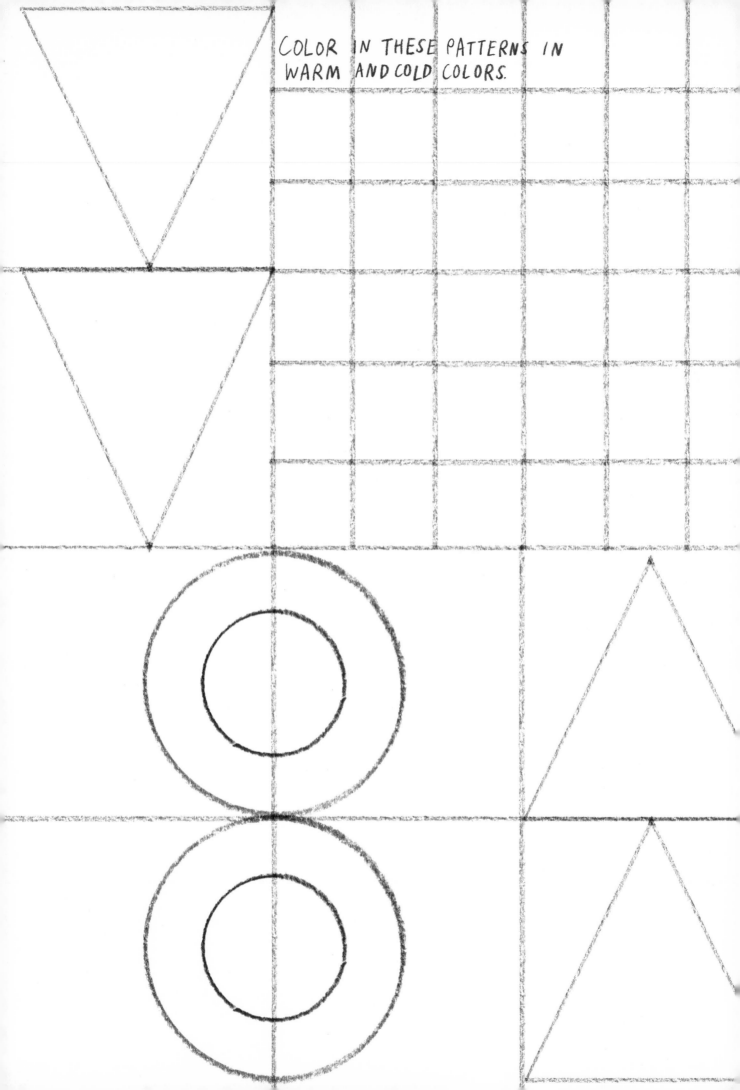

COLOR IN THESE PATTERNS IN WARM AND COLD COLORS.

COLOR

THE CIRCLES WITH BRIGHT PAINT OR FELT-TIP PENS.

BLACK

IS THE DARKEST COLOR. IT IS NOT
A WARM OR A COLD COLOR.
WE SEE BLACK WHEN NO VISIBLE
LIGHT REACHES THE EYE.

SPACE IS BLACK BUT IT IS FULL OF
STARS. USING A WHITE PEN, DRAW
THEM AND COLOR IN PLANET EARTH.